In My Spare Time

Poems by
Theodore A. Borrillo

© Copyright 2004
Theodore A. Borrillo
Littleton, Colorado
U.S.A.

All rights reserved

Names of individuals in any poems
are fictitious and are not intended to
represent any persons, living or dead.

ISBN 0-9744331-0-1

Acknowledgements

Graphic Design by Graham Poreda
Woodinville, Washington

Johnson Printing
1880 South 57th Court
Boulder, Colorado 80301

Happiness

is

often found

in

those choices

we make

in our spare time

CONTENTS

A Backward Life	1
The Rain in Venice	2
Airport Love	3
The Tour Bus to Acapulco	4
Book Advice	6
The Same Sky	8
Let's Stay in Touch	9
The Man on the Street Corner	11
Specks of Dust	13
The Dilemma of Old Castles	15
Unexpected Happenings	16
Make Something Beautiful Happen Today	18
Evening Reflection	20
A Lonely Day in Dublin	21
Reflections	23
A Young Woman in Berlin	25
On Being Present	26

Pretending	27
A Lot of Goodness	28
The Mothers at Daniel Park	31
Morgan's Land	32
How Can Anyone Be Sure of Love?	34
Seasonal Love	36
Above Autumn	37
Napoleon's Chair	38
The Corporate World of Jeremy Cantor	39
Was John Garfield Happy?	41
The Yangtze River is Brown	43
Hiroshima	45
Mary Schlossinger's Smiling Face	48
There's Nothing Wrong With Dreaming	49
Johnny Ryan's First Kiss	50
My Old Briefcase	53

Someone I Remember	55
The Haunting Image of the Homeless	57
I Should Have Known	59
I Welcome Summer's End	60
My Grandmother's Whispers	62
If	63
The St. Charles Avenue Streetcars	64
Gated Communities	65
Memories	66
An Old Man Who Lives on My Street	68
Last Night Was Cold and Wet	70
There Comes a Time	72
On Growing Older	73

A BACKWARD LIFE

If I had a choice
I'd live my life backwards
So youth would have
    the benefit
    of
    wisdom
    and experience
And old age would have
    no regrets

THE RAIN IN VENICE

It's been a long time since
    my first visit
    to Venice.
I remember the rain had
    scattered the tourists
    from the street
    outside the
    Teatro la Fenice
Where I had just seen
    Titus Andronicus
    performed by
    Laurence Olivier and
    Vivien Leigh.
I could hear the water
    gently splashing
    against
    the ancient buildings
    lined up along the canals.
I remember the candelabra-shaped
    street lamp
    that made the rain appear
    like silver threads
    dancing against
    the dark of night.
I will always remember those
    moments.
It may be the reason I like
    the rain.

AIRPORT LOVE

The world would be a better place
If people loved one another
With the fervor, the joy, and the
  embraces
Of those who say hello and goodbye
  at airports

THE TOUR BUS TO ACAPULCO

The tour bus to Acapulco
Slowed down
Long enough for the tour
    guide
To point out the mansion
    on the left
That overlooked
    the Gulf of Mexico
    and the mountains
And the long road to the
    iron gate
That let some people in
    and kept others out.
He said it belonged to
    Sylvester Stallone
The *Rocky* and *Rambo*
    movie star
But that he's seldom there
Because he has other places
    with other views
To satisfy his moods.

At that moment
I thought of the Bronx
    tenement flat where
    I was raised without
    a view
From where I could hear
    friendly voices
    from the stoop below
    of people chatting away
    the humid nights
    of summer,
And I remembered the
    oil-heated
    kitchen stove
    that kept us warm
    in winter
And how we huddled in
    the room
    before the
    evening meal
Sharing together the
    thoughts that each
    day brought.
There was love in
    the room
And I never thought of
    leaving.
I never thought of
    Acapulco.

BOOK ADVICE

When my son was a baby
My doctor gave me a book
     to read
       and it said
       that a baby,
       once put to bed,
       should not be picked up
       if he starts to cry,
As he may become
       demanding
       and spoiled.

But when I heard the baby
       cry
I picked him up
       and cradled him
       in my arms
       until he calmly
       slept again.
Then I put him down to
       dream away
       the night.

My son grew up to be a
       pediatrician
On the staff of a large
       hospital in
       Burlington, Vermont.

Now I baby-sit my son's son
and my son
showed me a book
that says
that a baby,
once put to bed,
should not be picked up
if he starts to cry,
As he may become
demanding
and spoiled.

But when I heard the baby
cry
I picked him up
and cradled him
in my arms
until he calmly
slept again.
Then I put him down to
dream away
the night.

And I looked down at him
and wondered
what he would
become.

THE SAME SKY

The earth rotates on its axis every
    twenty-four hours
And the sky that passes over Paris,
    France, is the same sky that passes
    over Tulsa, Oklahoma
But somehow, I would rather be in
    Paris

LET'S STAY IN TOUCH

It was nice seeing
    you today
    after all these
    years
    of our
    living in the same
    town
    not far from one
    another.

I thought you had
    moved
    to Kansas City!

It was nice seeing
    you today
Let's stay in touch.

Thank you for your
    business card.
I see that I can
    reach you at your
    web site
    or by e-mail
    or on your cell phone
    or by FAX.

On the other hand
   perhaps
   we might
   simply
   see each other
   some other time,
   surprisingly,
   like today,
   passing each
   other
   on a busy
   street corner.

Let's stay in touch.

THE MAN ON THE STREET CORNER

The man on the street corner
    stood in silence
    holding a violin
    which he played
    between resting,
    as passersby
    occasionally
    tossed a coin or two
    into
    a tattered hat
    while others walked by
    pretending not to see him.
I learned that he was from
    Sarajevo,
His home until the bombing
    and the devastation,
    until it was hard
    to remember
    what life was like
    before the war,
    before he became a
    refugee
In this land of many
    street corners.

He spoke little English
And was too old to learn
    to speak again
But the hands that held
    the violin
Were still young as
    his fingers danced
    upon the strings
And the bow sailed along
    the strains of music
    in the cold air of night
His eyes closed
In a state of sustained
    reverie
Perhaps dreaming of
    better days
    left behind
    or yet to come.

SPECKS OF DUST

The minute hand of my
    small silver clock
Stuttered back and forth,
    stuck in its forward
    movement.
I took it to a jeweler
    and watched
    as he brushed away
    a speck of dust
    that had lodged
    between the gears.
The minute hand again
    moved freely.

And so it can be said
    of people,
    frozen in their
    forward movement
By unresolved anger,
    by jealousy
    by envy
    by ego and
    selfishness that
    focus on matters
    causing them
    continual unrest
Those specks of dust
    that impede
    their progress
And mar their dignity.

THE DILEMMA OF OLD CASTLES

Old castles are cold and damp
Too historical to be abandoned
Too impractical to inhabit

UNEXPECTED HAPPENINGS

Sometimes life seems routine,
Like having a season ticket
    to baseball games.
The scores are different,
    and there is some
    variation in the
    chitchat of the
    nearby fans,
Yet there is a sameness
    to it all,
Like eating hot dogs and
    drinking beer and
    the seventh-inning
    stretch.

And then there are those
unexpected happenings
that I tell others
about,
Like winning a raffle for
a ride in a hot air
balloon,
Or staying two days in
Savannah
when the car
broke down,
Or falling in love with
Mercedes Cambridge,
the sales clerk who
sold me an umbrella
in New Orleans
on a rainy day.

MAKE SOMETHING BEAUTIFUL HAPPEN TODAY

Make something beautiful happen today
It need not be something that brings
    glory and fame
No headline achievement that mentions
    your name
Just a small deed for another in need
Before the day passes forever away.

Don't let the doomsayers get in your way
The ones who are quick to see everything
    blue
Know in your heart of the good you can do
Just share a smile more than once in a while
Make something beautiful happen today.

It's not as difficult as some make it seem
The world's full of heroes who have
    shown us the way
Who have given us courage to live out a
    dream
To make something beautiful happen each
    day.

So visit a friend whose life's gone astray
Without dreams or salvation as part of his
    plan
Make the sky bright for him, all day if you
    can
Just be sure to do what God wants you to
Make something beautiful happen today.

EVENING REFLECTION

lying awake
before sleeping,
thinking
in silence,
in the darkness of my room,
I ask myself
was what I did today
worth
a day of my life?

A LONELY DAY IN DUBLIN

I sat in an old theater in Dublin one night,
    just to waste away some time
    because I was alone and lonely.
I can't remember the name of the play I was
    there to see, but it didn't matter because
    I like the Irish and just about anything
    they write is good,
Even if it's not written by John Millington Synge.
I remember visiting Synge's grave that afternoon,
    and the cemetery attendant - not being sure
    if he was "the bloke who wrote about the
    playboy" - told me that few people ever asked
    to see his grave, and that's why he had
    trouble finding it.
I walked from the cemetery to the theater
    along a waterway, and I took my time because
    that's what lonely people do when there's
    no fancy that steals them away.
The theater used to be a music hall at the
    turn of the 19th century, and Charlie Chaplin
    performed there on November 19, 1900,
    almost a quarter of a century before
    Oona O'Neill would be born.
If there was anyone who could make me smile,
    it was Chaplin.

The play had its share of laughter and tears,
    as most Irish plays do, and as the lights
    of the theater came on, I noticed that I
    was one of the few people there alone.
I walked along the street towards my hotel to
    rest before my early morning flight home.
A thin fog had descended upon the city,
    embracing me,
    and my footsteps echoed
    in the stillness of the night,
    as though the city was listening,
As though Dublin knew that I'd come to share
    my loneliness with her.

REFLECTIONS

The restaurant around her was busy
    as she sat alone
    as though
    waiting
    for another
    to arrive,
    a special someone
    to share
    some moments together,
But no one came.
She was older than she looked
    at first glance.
She smiled as she spoke to the waiter.
It was her smile that made her appear
    more youthful,
At least for the moment, until
    her eyes revealed
    a restlessness
    that seemed
    to conceal regrets
    not to be talked about
    not to be shared
    not to interfere
    with her search
    for a new beginning.

As I looked at her from across the
    room, I sensed her sadness
    her longing
    her unfulfilled dreams
And I was reminded of my longings
    and empty dreams
As she became a mirror, reflecting
    my own loneliness.

A YOUNG WOMAN IN BERLIN

Heinke Walder is seated at
    an outdoor table
    of a Berlin cafe,
A young woman whose thoughts
    are of romance and life
    as she glances at
    the passersby,
As she waits for her lover,
While the lights of the
    boulevard
    highlight her beauty
    and the serenity
    of her composure
And music from a nearby cabaret
    punctuates the cool breezes
    of the summer night.
Heinke enjoys her life in today's
    Berlin,
And, as she gazes at the vitality
    of the city,
The devastation of 1945, the bombs,
    the rubble, the bunker,
    and Eva Braun,
    never enter her mind.

ON BEING PRESENT

I am aware that
    the strength and joy
    of life
    is found
    in being
    where you are,
    wherever the place,
    with whomever,
    listening,
    tracking the
    thoughts and
    feelings
    of the moment,
    letting go of yesterday
    not dreaming of tomorrow.

Still, there are times
    when I am in the
    mountains,
    I want to be by
    the sea,
    and when I am
    by the sea,
    I want to be in
    the mountains.
There are times when,
    by choice
    or distraction,
    I am not present.

PRETENDING

Where does the sky
    begin?
Where does it end?
Planets and stars
    floating
    in the endless
    universe
The earth spinning
    on its axis
Revolving around
    the sun
Turning night into
    day
And day into night
Forever dancing
    in space
As I tend to my
    garden
Pretending
    the world is flat
    the world is still.

A LOT OF GOODNESS

There's a lot of goodness in the world today
In spite of the economy and what politicians
    have to say
In spite of union strikes and the restless
    unemployed
In spite of all the prejudice and the wrongs
    we don't avoid
There is a lot of goodness and I'm sure it's
    here to stay.

There's a lot of goodness in the world today
I see it in a street sign that says
    "Children Here at Play"
I feel it every morning when a breeze blows
    up my walk
I hear it every Sunday when the preacher starts
    to talk
There is a lot of goodness if you fix your mind
    that way.

There's a lot of goodness in the world today
In Alaska and New Hampshire, and all
    along the way
In spite of the pollution and environmental
    woes
In spite of all the violence that pervades
    our movie shows
There is a lot of goodness and it's going to
    pass your way.

There's a lot of goodness in the world today
It's sitting right beside you, so you needn't
    have to stray
It's in somebody's prayer for you, it's in
    the sky above
It's in a baby's eyes, full of wonder,
    full of love
There is a lot of goodness, so don't look
    the other way.

THE MOTHERS AT DANIEL PARK

There was a time when I was young
And played in Daniel Park
And kicked a ball and climbed a tree
And laughed aloud 'cause I was free
As mothers watched like safety nets.

And now I'm old and hold a cane
To steady me as I walk by
At Daniel Park where children play
From time to time throughout the day
As mothers watch like safety nets.

Those memories of my youthful days
Are within my thoughts today
Of how I climbed and swung away
With my friends of yesterday.

My mother long has left this earth
As have my friends with whom I played
But Daniel Park lives now as then
And children smile as we did when
Our mothers watched like safety nets.

MORGAN'S LAND

Oliver Morgan was born
 and raised
 on a farm
 a few miles
 from a small town
 in Kansas.
He loves the flat land
 of Kansas
And the smell of the earth,
 far away from the sea.
He likes the sounds of
 the tractors
 in early morning
 as much as others
 like the sounds
 of birds.
He likes to shop in the
 country store on
 main street
 where people know him
 by name
 and talk about
 the crops
 that wait for rain.
And when the season is
 slow
 they put his purchases
 on a tab without
 him asking.

He doesn't suffer from
smog or
traffic jams.
Each day he watches the
sun rise
and the sun set,
and the bright red
colors
that light up the
sky and the land.

As a young schoolboy,
Oliver Morgan
learned
about big cities,
where skyscrapers
suffocate the land.
It made him love
his Kansas farmland
even more,
A land without skyscrapers,
A land yearning to be embraced
by the winter snow
the spring rain
the summer sky
And by the cool breezes
of autumn
at harvest.

HOW CAN ANYONE BE SURE OF LOVE?

There are as many
    reasons
    for love
As there are
    sunsets
    and
    songs
    illusions
    and deceptions

And so it happens
That two people
    fall in
    love
    almost
    without effort
Like two magnets
    drawn
    together
To be partners
    forever
    and ever
    for as long
    as the sun
    rises
    and the sun
    sets

To share dreams
    together
    forever
    and ever
    for as long
    as the waters
    of the
    Mississippi
    flow
    on and on
And then, almost
    without warning
Love may go astray
On lonely nights
    with
    wayward glances
Until two people
    fall out of
    love
Into the arms
    of others
    with
    different
    sunsets
    and
    songs
    illusions
    and deceptions

How can anyone be
    sure
    of love?

SEASONAL LOVE

Sometimes the leaves of autumn
        come too soon,
     before the summer's end,
     like an impatient lover

Sometimes the leaves of autumn
        stay too late,
     reluctant to leave,
     like an old lover

Sometimes an early snowstorm
        blankets
     the leaves of autumn
     chasing away a lover

Meanwhile, spring awaits us
     with fresh leaves
     and renewed hope
     for a steadfast love
     that may survive
        the seasons

ABOVE AUTUMN

I live in New York City
In a tall building
Above the lines of trees
Above autumn
And I think of you
In Colorado
Wandering on secluded
 paths
 among the trees,
 painted by windblown
 colors
 of gold and brown
Wandering peacefully
Watching the leaves
 of autumn
 waltz
 from treetops
Spiraling down to touch
 your face
 your lips
 embracing you,
As I once did, so long ago,
Before I foolishly left,
To live alone
Above the tree lines
Above autumn.

NAPOLEON'S CHAIR

The guide approached the room
　　of the Benedictine
　　monastery in Austria
　　with a solemnity
　　that silenced the
　　tourists.
The room was square and bare
　　except for a table
　　and chair
　　one could see
　　from behind a rope.
The guide explained that it was
　　Napoleon's chair,
Which looked too uncomfortable
　　for an emperor, as it was
　　just an ordinary chair.
The guide never mentioned the
　　table, only that
　　Napoleon spent one night
　　at the monastery
　　sometime in 1809
　　and sat in that chair,
　　where it has been ever since.
I took a photograph of the
　　chair but did not
　　include it in my album,
　　preferring instead a photograph
　　I took of the Danube River,
　　which was also in Austria
　　sometime in 1809.

THE CORPORATE WORLD OF JEREMY CANTOR

Jeremy Cantor was ambitious
and taught to measure
success in life
by his place on
the corporate ladder
and by the size of his
stock options portfolio.
He learned the importance of
net worth, profit, and
cut-throat competition.
He supported cost-cutting
practices of downsizing
and early retirement
policies.
As time passed, his competitive
drive permeated every
aspect of his life,
until there was no balance
to his existence, but
only winners and losers.
He became insensitive to
his family waiting
each day
for the long work hours
to end,
which never did.

Jeremy Cantor didn't seem to
    have any interest in the
    many ordinary and simple
    day-to-day pleasures
    of living, consumed as
    he was with business deals
    and balance sheets.
Years later,
    his marriage dissolved,
    and his children strangers,
    he sat in his executive office,
    never wondering whether
    he had mistaken success
    for happiness, for he had
    become the CEO,
    a winner,
    surrounded by himself.

WAS JOHN GARFIELD HAPPY?

I often wonder if John Garfield
    was happy.
I just assumed that he was because
    he was a film star
And made a movie with Joan Crawford.
I liked Joan Crawford.
Then I read *Mommie Dearest*, and I
    learned that Joan Crawford
    wasn't happy.
And that's when I began to wonder
    about John Garfield.
I learned that he grew up
    in New York's tough
    Lower East Side
And that John Garfield
    wasn't his real name.
He attended a school for problem
    children.
He was blacklisted by
    the House Committee
    on Un-American Activities
For refusing to name friends as
    communists
During the tainted turmoil of the
    '50s.
He died from a heart attack at the
    age of 39.

I began to realize that happiness
    isn't always measured
    by success
Or by getting to kiss Joan Crawford
    in a movie
Or by having your picture on the
    cover of a movie magazine.
Rather, it's something inside that
    isn't visible
Like peace of mind and soul.
I wonder if John Garfield was happy?
The Fallen Sparrow was one of his
    films.

THE YANGTZE RIVER IS BROWN

The Yangtze River is brown
As brown as the desert sands of Arizona.
Mile after mile,
The river's always brown, brown, brown.
There's no use wishing it to be another
    color
Because it just won't change.
It's as stubborn as the currents of the
    Mississippi.
It's as mighty as the dragons of China.
People just call it *"the river,"* because
    there's nothing else like it,
Like the Great Wall of China is just
    "the wall."
I sat and watched the Yangtze day after
    day
Staring at it, as I would a painting I
    couldn't understand.
After a while the river took me in,
And I knew that I wouldn't change it,
    even if I could.
The river was meant to be brown
Like the hills that surround it are
    meant to be green
And the sky above it is meant to be blue.

HIROSHIMA

The conference in Tokyo ended.
I was scheduled to return home,
But, instead, I was drawn to visit Hiroshima
And felt powerless to resist.
The image of the mushroom cloud over Hiroshima
That I saw in newsreels when I was a child
Beckoned me there.

The bullet train from Tokyo sped along
     the countryside
     as I strained to prepare myself
     for the visit.
The beauty of Hiroshima greeted me
     as I walked along its boulevards
     of fancy hotels
     and fine department stores
     and gentle people
     busily going about their daily work
          and chores
     much like Americans on Madison Avenue
     thousands of miles away.
As I approached the bomb site,
I passed within a few feet of the
     only building
     whose stone frame
     partially withstood the bomb,
     a shattered relic,
     a reminder
     of the senseless tragedies of war.

I began to feel lightheaded.
I could not control the throbbing of
    my heart.
I stepped into the area where the bomb
    had exploded on August 6, 1945
    at 8:15 in the morning
    over thousands
    of people going to work.
The site is now a large park of shrines
    and monuments
    in memory of those who died.
Further into the park was a museum,
    and I entered and viewed
    photographs that depicted
    the horrors and devastation
    from the bomb.
The city resembled a human ash tray.
There were photographs of burnt bodies,
    of scarred and twisted faces,
    from
    the unexpected confrontation
    with death and suffering.
A group of young students entered the
    museum,
    led by their teacher
    who began to describe
    the day that changed the world.

The image of the bomb as I had seen it
    as a child
    surfaced in my mind
    as I stood before
    those children,
Feeling guilty with no rational
    explanation that could
    absolve me of my feelings.
The moment opened a wound that I knew
    would never heal.
I left the museum and walked about the
    park,
    praying at some of the shrines
    and monuments,
    and then leaving;
Again, towards the boulevards that were
    so friendly.
And as I left the area, I saw the name
    given to the site,

      PEACE PARK

MARY SCHLOSSINGER'S SMILING FACE

Trying to smile is not easy for some
    people
They smirk when the photographer says,

    "chee - ee - se"

Because it's hard for them to break
    into a broad smile.
It isn't that they're unhappy or sad,
It's just that they were not born with
    a smiling face.
You know what I mean.

But there are others,
Like Mary Schlossinger.
She smiles immediately upon contact.
You could be talking about a funeral
    or the latest war,
    or the stock market crash,
And Mary Schlossinger's face becomes
    a smile.
It's not that she's disingenuous.
It's just that her face is configured
    to smile.
And she looks happy.
In fact, I don't remember when she
    ever looked sad.

I always think of Mary Schlossinger
    whenever the photographer says,

    "chee - ee - se"

THERE'S NOTHING WRONG WITH DREAMING

I often think of what I'd like to be
    but never was
It's not that I'm unhappy about who
    I am or what I do,
It's just that life's too short for
    all our dreams.
We choose a line of work too soon
    and hope it's right,
Then lead our lives wondering if there
    was something else we missed.

Everyone loves to dream of being someone
    else in his imagination,
Like playing the role of Murray Burns
    in *A Thousand Clowns*,
(I was really good as Columbus in a
    seventh grade play),
Or being a third baseman in the major
    leagues,
Or a sports writer for *The Boston Globe*.

It's fun to dream and I guess it's safe
    to say
There's nothing wrong with dreaming,
    because things rarely
    go wrong in dreams,
    as they often do in life.

JOHNNY RYAN'S FIRST KISS

Johnny Ryan is like most people,
   in that he remembers
   things he did in life
   for the first time,
Like seeing his first Broadway play
   from the balcony of
   the New Century Theatre
   where Phil Silvers
   and Nanette Fabray
   sang and danced
   in *High Button Shoes,*
Or like his first journey in
   a military transport,
   crossing the English Channel
   almost within reach
   of the cliffs of Dover.
Or like his first kiss at seventeen.

Grace Riley was twenty-two and
   worked in the sales department
   where he was an office boy.
She was tall, and as she walked,
   her arms moved gracefully
   in rhythm with her slender figure.

Grace took the same subway line home,
    and soon they rode the train
    together.
Standing close to her, he was
    enraptured by the scent
    of her perfume.
He sometimes got off at her stop,
    walking a few blocks
    to where she lived
    before taking a bus home.

Johnny never shared his feelings
    of affection for her
    because it was an awkward
    first for him,
    as she was older,
    and just a casual friend
    who rode the same
    train line home.
On one of the walks from the train
    station, a sudden burst of
    rain forced them into the
    narrow entryway of a store
    that had closed for the night.
They stood alone face to face
    listening to the rain,
    while the soft glow of
    an evening street light
    invited them to kiss,
    as though it were part
    of some movie scene.

There was no passionate embrace,
     just the tenderness
     of a kiss,
     like two old friends
     who meet,
     then softly say goodbye,
     but nothing more.
It was Johnny Ryan's first kiss.

A week later Johnny left for
     college in the Midwest.
He became a structural engineer
     and designs buildings in
     San Francisco to make them
     earthquake safe.
He never saw Grace Riley again,
     and there's a chance she
     might remember him if
     someone jogged her memory,
But whenever Johnny returns to
     New York, he brings himself
     before that narrow entryway
     where life began to unravel
     in the heart
     of a seventeen-year-old.

MY OLD BRIEFCASE

At a book signing, a man
    said to me
    that poets
    can write
    about anything
And he picked up my old
    and battered
    leather briefcase
And said, "I bet that you
    could even
    write a poem
    about
    this briefcase."

He must have sensed that
    my worn-out
    briefcase
Was as much a part of me
As the memories I harbor
For the briefcase held
    many secrets
From agenda books that
    mapped
    my history,
To thoughts of love that
    shaped
    my life
    my writing.

As I wondered how he sensed
    it all
He handed me the briefcase,
    gently,
    with an aura
    of reverence
And it was then I knew
    it was because
    he had
    the heart
    of a poet.

SOMEONE I REMEMBER

I hadn't seen her for a long
　time.
Often I wondered what became
　of her.
She was a classmate of mine
　when we were
　in our teens
　in Manhattan.
She was smart and fun to be
　with and wanted
　to become a doctor
　and talked about
　going to Columbia University.
Then she won a contest and
　became
　the beauty queen
　for a wine festival
　in California
And never returned
　to Manhattan.
I kept a photograph of her
　that appeared in
　the *Daily News*
　showing her smiling
　when being crowned
　beauty queen.
Later I heard she played
　bit parts in some
　B-movies
And married an actor she met
　on the lot.

I just assumed that things
    took off for her
    because
    she was smart
    and attractive
    and determined
    to succeed.
But that's all I knew of her
    for many years.
Last week, I read a story
    in a Los Angeles
    newspaper
    that a former
    beauty queen and starlet
    in B-movies
    overdosed on drugs
    and died.
And it was she,
    only 39 years old,
    and no longer beautiful.
There was no mention of any
    family.
It was a pathetic story by
    a Hollywood
    gossip columnist
    feasting upon
    another's misfortunes.
It made me cry because I knew
    her worth.

THE HAUNTING IMAGE OF THE HOMELESS

I saw him leaning against
   a building
   to avoid
   the sudden burst
   of rain
   that washed
   the summer streets
   in sunlight.
He was dressed shabbily
   in worn-out clothes
   holding
   a cardboard sign
   that said
   HOMELESS, HELP ME
   MAY GOD BLESS YOU

Most passed him by
    as though he were
    invisible, certain
    he was just
    another drunk
    begging
    between drinks,
When the thought
    occurred to me
    that the God who
    created him
    is the same God
    who created
    Michelangelo
    Mother Teresa
    and
    Martin Luther King.

The seasons pass on
    and on
But the image of him
    holding a sign
    asking God
    to bless me
    is ingrained
    in my memory.

I SHOULD HAVE KNOWN

things didn't work
out
today

it was a bad day
notwithstanding that

the gas station
    attendant
the postal clerk
the waiter
the bank teller
the pharmacist
and the sales clerk
    at Saks

all said to me

HAVE A NICE DAY!

I WELCOME SUMMER'S END

I welcome summer's end
    as much as I awaited its beginning,
    because summer gets too hot and long at times.
It's then I begin to yearn for autumn,
    for the cool breezes that tell me
    winter is coming,
    and that I should gather logs for the fireplace.
The fire's glow
    is softer than that of the summer sun,
    glowing at the end of day,
    when telephones are still,
    and children comfortably asleep.
I welcome summer's end and longer nights,
    and the warmth and peace
    of a fire's glow.

MY GRANDMOTHER'S WHISPERS

The meaning of life comes in whispers
Like the stories my grandmother told
When I was a young boy in Kansas
And the nights were windy and cold.

I haven't read every book I own
And I've never seen a Broadway play
I haven't kissed every girl I've known
And I've never been to Santa Fe.

I've never seen the Cote d'Azur
And I doubt if I ever will
Or the Palace of the Popes in Avignon
Where the world is quiet and still.

But life isn't measured by the things
    you don't do
Nor by the many things you don't see
Be it *Carousel* on a Broadway stage
Or the gardens of Monet in Giverny.

My meaning of life came from whispers
From the stories my grandmother told
When I was a young boy in Kansas
And the nights were windy and cold.

IF

If a day had only 20 hours
    instead of 24
We would have a longer life
    expectancy
But would look older at 70
    than we now do

THE ST. CHARLES AVENUE STREETCARS

The St. Charles Avenue streetcars still thread their way
    through the streets of New Orleans
    as they have for decades,
Vintage olive-green colored streetcars with wooden seats,
    clanging bells, and windows that open
Upon tracks that were laid in 1835.
The St. Charles Avenue streetcars provide the arterial
    stamina and energy of the city
Where 23,000 residents ride them on an average workday
Moving through neighborhoods of southern mansions,
    and street corners of jazz musicians
    and gaping tourists.
New Orleans is where I go when I find myself caught in
    the flow of a world that refuses to stand still,
A world that seems to change too fast, without permission,
    without reflection, and sometimes just for the sake
    of change.
It's then I remember the stability and sanity of the past
    as I ride all afternoon to and from Canal Street
    on the streetcars that travel on St. Charles Avenue.
If New Orleans abandoned its vintage streetcars for
    modern transportation
It would become a city that skips a heartbeat
Like a St. Louis without the Mississippi River
A Denver without the Rocky Mountains
Or a New York without a skyline.
Thankfully, the St. Charles Avenue streetcars and the city
    are committed to preserving the charm
    of days gone by,
    of a slower world,
    where friends have time to say hello.

GATED COMMUNITIES

Gated communities
Are a form of discrimination
Under the guise of security
By people
Who go to church on Sunday
To pray
For those less fortunate

MEMORIES

There was a factory by the river
Near my house beside the mill
At the outskirts of a city
In a world where time stood still
The people there were friendly
In a cheerful sort of way
And life was so much simpler
Than the life I have today.

My early years were blessed
And I welcomed every day
Never thinking time could change
That place of yesterday.
Then I became a man
And made my way alone
To seek my fortune in a world
So different than the one I'd known.

Life travels now at a rapid pace
There isn't time along the way
To let my mind just wander free
To soothe the stresses of each day.
There is distance all around me
The simple life has given way
To tensions of the quest to win.
Gone is the warmth of yesterday.

The factory's now an empty relic
Standing by the river's flow
There are strangers in the garden
Of the house I used to know.
There are no memories left to grasp
Except those of long ago
Those joyful days when I was young
And could watch the flowers grow.

AN OLD MAN WHO LIVES ON MY STREET

There's an old man who lives on my street
    whom I seldom see
And when I do he never speaks to me,
Or to others, for that matter,
Not out of hatred or disregard;
It's just the way he is
All to himself
Perhaps preoccupied about matters that I
    will never know
And should never ask.

Some say he's aloof
But perhaps he's just old and has probably
    heard most
      of what people have to say.
So much that is said today is unnecessary or
    redundant
How often have we said things we later felt
    would have been better left unsaid
Words that hurt or were misunderstood or
    untrue
And there is that awful gossip talk that's
    none of our business.

There is an old man who lives on my street
    whom I seldom see
And when I do he never speaks to me,
Not out of hatred or disregard;
Some say he's aloof
But perhaps he's wiser than most and knows
    that silence is golden
    and believes that time and words
    should not be wasted on
    meaningless conversations.

LAST NIGHT WAS COLD AND WET

I wondered where he slept last night
For the ground was cold and wet from
    an early season snowstorm.
Before now, I hadn't thought much
    about him
      except that he was one of
      the many homeless
      on street corners
      with a cardboard sign
      and outstretched hands.
I got used to seeing him on the
    same corner,
      like one sees a concession stand
      offering things no one needs.
So I just looked and passed him by.

It's natural not to become involved
    in another's world.
It's wise to be careful about
    who we take in and
    who we keep out.
That's what gated communities are all
    about.

I wondered where he slept last night
For the ground was cold and wet from
    an early season snowstorm.
And then I saw him.
The morning edition of the *Daily Times*
    had a photograph of him
    stretched out along the
    edge of an office building
    on the sidewalk
    along twentieth street,
His head lying on the cardboard sign
    as if upon a pillow.
He was dead.
There was no mention of his name or
    where he was from.
He was just a photograph in a story
    about the early snowstorm
    and of the need
    to keep warm,
For the ground was cold and wet.

THERE COMES A TIME

There comes a time as parents
When we must say
That it's okay
For our children to grow up
And go away
For them to start a world alone
To find their way
In a city that suits their fancy
Day by day
However far that place may be
We must believe
They'll be okay.

There comes a time for us to say,
However difficult it be,
That they're no longer children
And must be free!

ON GROWING OLDER
(to Elfriede)

I have never seen you growing older
Day by day you look the same to me
As beautiful and still as the river Meuse
Which never seems to flow, although it does.

This book is for my grandchildren, with love.

Nicolas Richard Borrillo
Mario Antonio Borrillo
and
Stella Yên Borrillo

Theodore A. Borrillo, the author,
was born in New York City,
and now resides in Littleton, Colorado
with his wife, Elfriede.

Other Poetry Books by the Author

Beyond Loneliness
Random Thoughts for Rainy Days